Whispers of TRUTH

WRITTEN BY
LORNA LEILANII

For my Husband Peter

In every pearl of wisdom
There is a grain of sand, a diamond, a rock!
The treasures in the sand we seek, simply speak of one momentous pleasure
.....TIME WITH YOU.....
Thank you for being my rock, my time with you - In Love

To our daughters

Lahara, Sahlua, and Nyantara

Thank you for the insights we could not have seen without you, the lessons we could not have learned except through you, and the profound understandings of "Truth" that speak of an inevitable bigger picture to life - expectation to revelation, participant to observer, and the poignant moments that take us from attachment to release...

Omni Avincent Amore our daughters,

Love Conquers All

Copyright © 2019 by Lorna Leilanii. 513755

ISBN:
Softcover   978-1-5144-9470-7
EBook   978-1-5144-9471-4

Print information available on the last page.

Rev. date: 07/30/2019

To order additional copies of this book, contact:
Xlibris
1-800-455-039
www.xlibris.com.au
Orders@Xlibris.com.au

To sit in the seat of non judgement
Is to experience life's mysteries
Journey the shoals of the soul
And hear innate wisdoms
That teach us to grow

Love Is

Its seed is my anchor
Its growth accommodates so many
Its journey, mystery and discovery
Its joy, abundance in every little blessing

Its glow, ignites me with courage and desire
To be more than I am and all I can be
It is the beacon in the darkest night

With every breath it fills me
With it comes the gift to give
With the gift to give is the gift to love, unconditionally

For life is truly precious

Preparing The Way

Submissions of thanks to those gone before
Stewarding me for ways of a law
Keeping me safe in a world all about
Where nature and man cannot live without
Shelter and seeding and growing our words
Lifting our mindset with voice of man heard
Houses unfolding to shade from the sun
Plans for a species that have yet to come
Land and the water and sky up above
For those still behind me just so much to love
Submissions of thanks for blessings of day
And night lights for rest, to nest and to pray

First Love We Sew

To you who created me into my being
With love, discipline, future unseen
Your cultures I am blessed
Great horizons for me
I have been built from Papuan Maori
The doors you have opened
Walk through with great stride
Your precious values forever my guide.

(With special mention of my parents, Flora and Te Rangatahi, for their love, courage, endurance, and those gone before preparing the way with love)

The Many Faces of Love

Love of Mum and Dad, the first love we sew
The mystery, the awe, of things that they know
The promises of life or to have things galore
Such hunger to fill as our needs want more
Our bodies then start a language their own
Chemically, sensory, flesh on fire
The brain makes no sense, now its desire

The day does come beyond love of Mum and Dad
To serve and share in life the gifts from their pad
And more from this world to new places sought
The gift that is you, different ways, different thoughts
Designed to be special for another cause

Love has a call, lust or in need
A choice we make, or just loyalty
To who or to what or somewhere to hide
Until love's truth brings true love alive
For you, of yourself, how many years gone
To find the love you caught was someone else' song

Be it spouse, be it children, many faces love is sought
Many gifts, many dollars, many powers love is brought
But of the many faces love is said to come
From the gentle hand of God there is only one

The one that never changes stays consistent through the years
Quietly it holds us and takes us through our fears
Just a feeling, always trusting, always knowing it's the one
Like cupid's arrow deep within, the love that leads us home

Is truth, your truth, be the carver within
The dancer or the angel or the Mr Fix-it man
In the jungle of emotion, in the desert where you stand
The joy that keeps you breathing, the smile your flame expands
The face of love that lights the way,
A gentle breath that fills each day
Only your heart knows the answer, only your soul knows its plan

In Truth

Dance of Life

We are all participants in the dance of life
Dancing our rhythm on a designated platform responding to someone else' tune
To better understand ourselves, or, on mission, to create a new tune for someone else to evolve

Our dance of life is unquestionably impacted by the elements
When it is hot we open up like flowers to absorb warmth or even dance a higher step
For the heat under our feet in the ferocity of storms puts anger in our hearts, and resistance
We plough through our dance with impatience knocking others over
Making ourselves unapproachable and time-out is needed
When the rhythm of joy sends us swirling and singing we will lick in the rain without dampening our spirit
Wear its wet elements clothed in love and retreat from its torrents
Exuding the sunshine that glows from within, it fills us

The elements are our guardians, here before us and puppets to a higher order
Earth, fire, wind, and water
Is it possible they too are here to experience their form and in mission with their function
Is it possible our experiences are like the many facets of a crystal with one portion of us shining to the sun
As the elements work our other facets grinding, charring, and lifting us out of the mire to a new design
Shaping us for our destiny and a higher vibration

There is purpose for us
Purpose for the elements and purpose for our interaction
There is personality in the higher order which orchestrates the dance of life
Such is the tiny star that evolves to brilliance
Shining its light into eternity

Portals

Spirits journey in portals of flesh
Shaping their souls to heights of success
Fluttering butterflies, insects of kind
Whispering breezes, ticking of time
Energy shaped, energy free
Workings of love, time to be

The breath of life an eternal flame
Radiates truly in all domains
Acceptance of self, non judgement begins
True love expanding from within
Bright is the light to all it serves
From breaths of truth our paths emerge

Follow the light that leads the way
The soul, the joy, the is each day
Forever within, forever with more
The portals now framed, are keys to a door

To Love

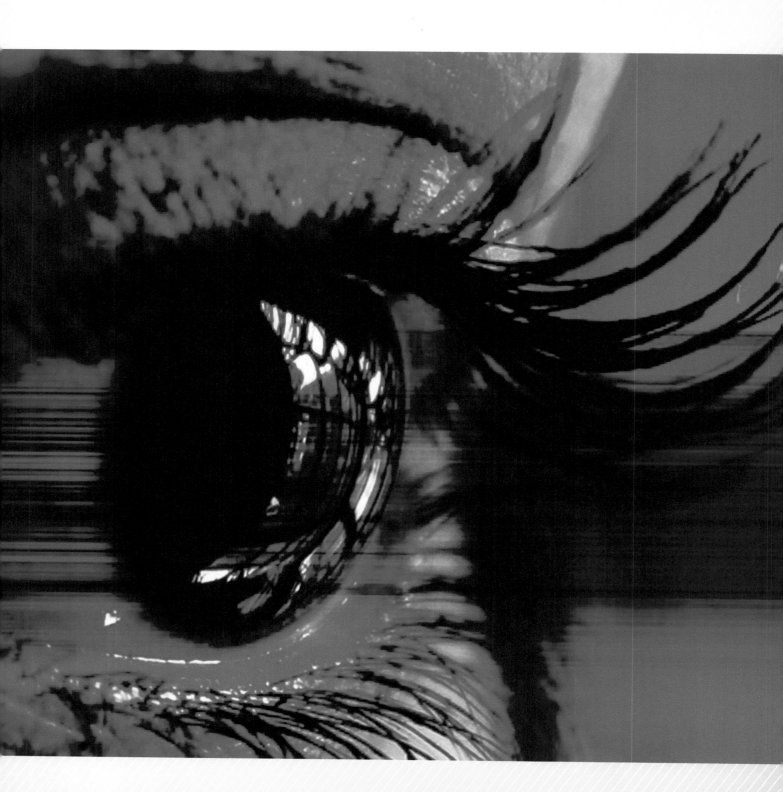

Free to Fly

I am who I am, but who am I
I am what I am, but what am I
I am where I am, but where am I
Beneath this universal sky

Be God, be Buddha, be any name
Show me to be someone with no shame
The body that is, is not mine anymore
I've handed it over and you have the door

Somewhere is I, somewhere is me
Somewhere within my integrity
Be awkward, be silly
Be oh so naive
A brain, yes I have but no memory
Like a stumbling foal from a stallion past
It's okay to be me each day from the last

Through this I will go
With your patience, support
Without judgment my heart can be free to talk
So hear me my friends to the heart that is me
Give the soul that is I time to be
So I can find the me that is I
And my spirit will shine free to fly

Time With You

Treasures in the sand we seek

Simply Speak of One Momentous Pleasure

.....TIME WITH YOU.....

Rhythms of Time

I looked in the heart of an old man today
I heard not his words, just his eyes that did say
Something to fathom, too slow to work out
Through the bright light of hope as his heart reaches out

You stopped for me lady, know not who you are
Stay with me longer and help this old heart
A bright smile is all that I need for today
Been a while since a lady smiled to me this way
The menu, you ask, what would I like for tea
Soup, with a salad and pie just for me
You can't stop, unjumble the words that won't come
Too busy I know far too much to be done

Lunchtime, maybe, or this afternoon
Hope that a word will come calling soon
The bright spark of hope, how long can it last
A moment or two of your time goes so fast
But the imprint of love in a smile from the heart
…...Stretches to eternity…..

Re - Birth

The rage of fire's onslaught, simply to destroy! Think again
The might of mother nature – primitive
Arduous in her grandeur evokes the elements into courtship
Re-aligning to her desire creating new life

The air is pregnant
Heavy in oils of eucalypt awaiting storm to deliver in an otherwise sterile land
Her moans begin in thunder rolls
Excited the wind howls carrying the fervor of new life when nature's match is lit
Lightning strikes an explosive mix erupting fire's unleashed desire
He has raped the land as she lies open in his remnants

Rain spills
Soothing, feeding, blending, kneading, earth draws him in
Storm departs and nature rests
Sunshine smiles spreading her arms of warmth
Nurturing fresh nutrient and re-growth, the land lives again

Man takes from my belly his caesarian wide and deep
He creates from that he taketh but even my gifts have their time to return home
Man holds on fighting so we struggle
My wrath is great as I re-cycle
Articulating what is mine to return to my belly
And, re-birth

Night Vision

Sharp snaps sear the air
Fire draws, flames appear
Eyes awake from eyes asleep
Danger in the house entreats

Like bolts of lightning, out of bed
From left to right I turn my head
No smoke is swirling through the air
Don't understand that picture there

Into each room run for my girls
Daughters three asleep are curled
And there beside a wall it stands
Too close it sits, as if commands
The paint it blisters in her heat
Calls echoing a quick retreat
Safely from a fiery sleep
I wheel it out, the heater by the wall

Taps are opened, towels are plunged
As through the morn that wall I sponge
Until my husband home he comes
Night Vision…. .. … .. … a fiery wall now dormant!

Sisters

The days we spent together I recall clear as light
When happiness shone from our hearts
Tears when dwelling on the past, we reminisce
When anger raged, a muttered glare
A saucepan lid – CRASH – on the floor
We meant business, twould be more

Then, softly, not too soon
Twould hum a tune I would
From in my soul out on my tongue would roll
A sad song at first, melancholy
Echoing my heart's lament where from our fight
Our love we bent

From my tune you find yourself drawn
Such peculiar sounds we could not help perform
Would send us laughing into the morn

My sisters I do thank you so
For all our love shared long ago, and yesterday
Tomorrow my heart holds you bound
In all the todays my life shall find

Forever. . . . .

Prison Socks

At the door she stands aghast
The key does not return the clasp
And light is low her vision dim
A frantic effort to get in

Sounds of footsteps, darkened sky
No melody of lullaby
Shaking fingers try again to no avail
Now burdensome
A heavy thud is closing in, must change the key

An evil grin now closes round the metal shaft
Tormenting a sweaty grasp
Then sliding round the knob does turn
Falling through her stomach churns
A nauseous wrenching of her gut
She desperately slams it shut
An uncontained sludge spills below the door
And as she falls, reveals a rising glow

A slow and shuffled sound retreats
She breathes the odour she has reached
Her pallor white, a fearful chill
Adrenalin no more a thrill
Secure now behind her locks
Her joy, her wealth, her prison socks!

Lady

Through this gift of luscious grace
Her knotted woods in strong embrace
Reaching from her solid girth
An embryo of our sweet earth
She clambers for the sky above
With leathered leaves to shield a dove

For lovers of a waking morn
Her splendor for your house adorns
Inviting aromatic beans of coffee
By an open sea

Across the globe her seekers come
For shelter from a blazing sun
With arms outstretched she looks beneath
From hills to shore
Lady of the landscape
They meet and greet with you

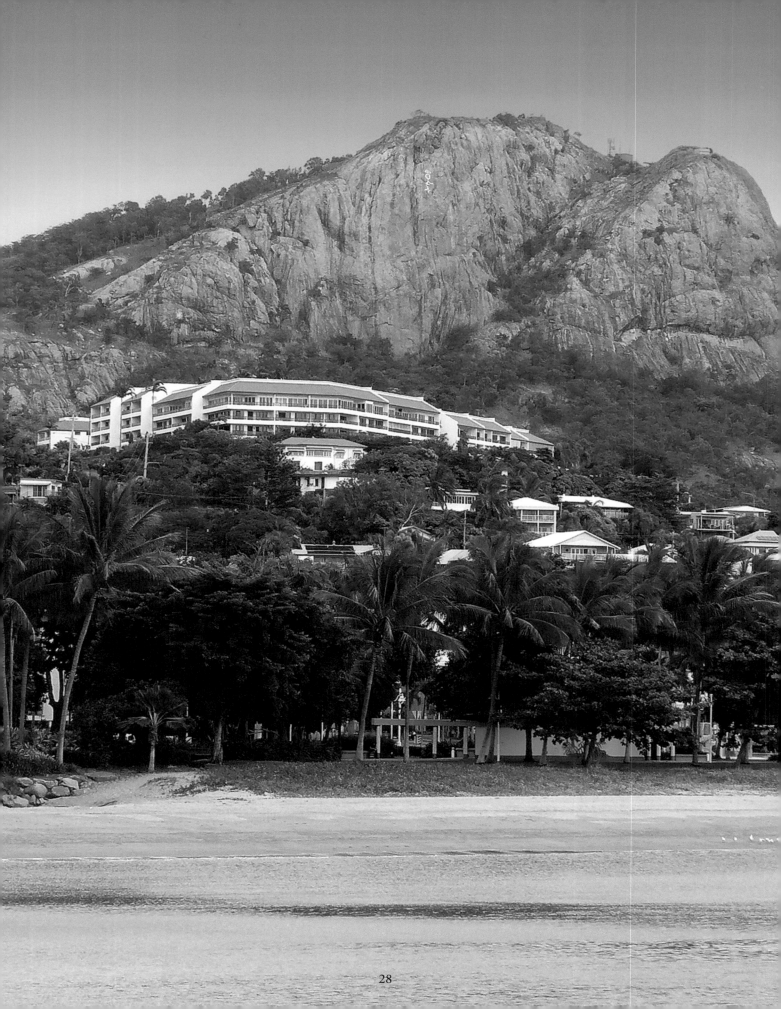

Castle Hill

Somewhere in the shadows
A little day or night
A butterfly emerges
She's taking her first flight

Somewhere in the shadows
A little morning sun
They're coming up the mountain
About to take a run

Somewhere in the shadows
Their eyes must lift and glance
A snake slithers slowly
On the rock of second chance

Somewhere in the shadows
High above their reach
The kiss of rain through canopy
And songs of birds retreat

Somewhere in the shadows
This castle calls her knights
Their shoes, their shorts, their shirts take wings
To lift them into flight

Heartbeat of a city
For some a climb assault
The passion of their footwork
Massage her with their trod

Somewhere in the shadows
A pounding fleet of feet
They've conquered round and ragged slopes
This castle from the street

Shadows To The Sun

For Caine

Her scream is stilled in her throat. Her heart frozen she chills at a voice somewhere in her head. Confused, her eyes seeing a perfect sunny blue sky through her window Francesca cannot compute the grey fog, bleak and surreal, as her voice rings out "NO....." Lifting her feet she begins to run. Hold on my darling the fight's just begun. What is this game plan, unprepared, no rules? Calling her husband, "please come home, collect the girls from school. My brother is dying and have to take my tools", as she gathers her books in case they change the rules and allow her to administer medicines new. That call. That moment in time when the world stops and life has frozen. When death from a sentence cannot compare to death from a life lost, from your own! A battle ensues for preservation through effort and hope.

What they see is magic each hour he responds, the specialists and their machines they pray for a song. When day two brings his heartbeat we all celebrate, his family, friends, fiancée too but all has come too late. A momentary promise, "Cheers!" from deep within, this six-foot four yet twenty-five, strength of man has said goodbye. A gentle heart, exquisite grin, and life snuffs short his flame within, no knowing why - his clock has stopped!

Day three at his battle's end, all quietly reflect, the time he had no heartbeat till the Ambo's gave him breath, day one of this call of death. There as he lay comatose, Mum and Dad time to let go, my sisters too I love you so, and nieces. Forgive me for this early close yet love inside is truly full with you. A lily close so very near, and love's perfume is heaven scent till Summer comes crystal clear, and so goodbye my dears.

Their September has grasped the weeks. The intensity of pain around her family has not ebbed. A lead-like weight, unfeeling in the wake has dragged them through one senseless day into another, this October day no different, yet it is. Francesca steps outside under the patio and she can feel the sun. There isn't a cloud in the sky and a familiarity returns. Although not in flower, the birds are in the jasmine tree and Francesca has not heard them before. A soft gurgling musical sound in short triplets. It is the first time she is truly alone since her nightmare call to critical care to be with her brother. He is at peace. Francesca's thoughts reach for an unseen angel, her guardian through the valley of death, the medicine man of homeopathy who fought for them as their last resort and who prayed for them.

When in the depths of sorrow comes a glimmer of light
For hope released in knowledge new is comfort through its plight

Contemplating the medicinal actions of her remedies and the cornerstone that held her upright through the sojourn - her husband, a brighter story entered as Francesca recalls her dream.

Warmed inside and out to the reaches of her fingers and toes, the magnificence of white magnolias arch in front of her. A white dove and bluebird fly through and around swooping, beckoning

onto a clearing of green grass beyond. Aware of her bare feet as she sinks into a soft cool damp, Francesca's stride quickens toward a break in the earth of white pebbles, river-stones and crystals as a bed to a gentle stream. An enormous rainforest rises either side and in front of her. Without fear she steps onto the streambed and in its meander becomes aware two angels have joined her. Now she is annoyed as it is her brother she wants to see but they have come instead. Not only does she feel disappointed but is uncomfortable with her annoyance at her holy guides. Onward past sounds of breaking foliage, the occasional hum of insects and sometimes just the sound of her own breathing, her angels do not speak.

Soon enough, a large river boulder appears for rest. Smooth and dry a stop is acknowledged as Francesca lays herself outstretched supporting her now weary frame on the surprisingly comfortable outcrop. As the light flickers through the foliage Francesca is sure she sees her brother across the stream leaning against a pillar of bark and holding a conch shell. Her conscious mind tells her she has willed him there and as if reading her thoughts her master angel raises his wing in front of her, obscuring any possibility of viewing him. Respectfully, she understands she must not hold onto him with her selfish desires to the earth plane, releasing him to heal on his journey to God's kingdom. As if trusted not to violate such a fragile guard as an understanding, Francesca's angels vanish through a parting of the canopy high above her head, releasing a golden ray of light accenting her journey home. Assuming this was so and in a prayer of release, her angels return to take her home, except, Francesca is escorted further into the magnificent, intense, yet serene rainforest.

Spellbound to see emerging from a clearing the iridescence of a blue crustacean, almond eyes peer out from under, hooded by curved sharp edges and side-way gait the invitation to follow is heeded. A change of focus forced by the unexpected presence of matter directly above, the gel of air moving, shining, it was alive. As it hovered a rise of excitement propelled Francesca forward to catch the presence of matter as the invisible force spilled out breathtaking colour and size of giant butterflies, insects and fairies in playful abound. As quickly as a glimpse can catch a rainbow in the overhead spray of a garden, they took their colony to find another sunbeam, Francesca could only guess. A few more steps and around a bend she gasped at the force of a cascading waterfall, a power unheard for the density of forest revealing an abundance of flowers, the playground for the colony of life-forms she had chanced upon moments before. Without notice, the angels lifted her. High on top the enormity of caves from which the awe of waterfall spilled she was left alone. Above, below, and around, from within the expanse of abundant life Francesca breathed all that was, within. Tranquil in the stillness its hum echoed her existence back on that mountain top, a portal of angelic light, Francesca knew she had found God's kingdom. To see, to know, to be. Framed in her archway of magnificent magnolias, her white dove and bluebird excited she had found their Eden, Francesca awoke.

"Now on his journey I know where he goes, with angels to guide him and show me where souls from the shadows of life are brought to the sun, Christ's promise to love and lead us home. From wretched loss comes a brand-new dawn, redemption revealed, in surrender we mourn. Here is a gift of heavenly grace that we can share such a magical place, and reach within His gift to receive, the kingdom of God for you and for me."

Through his dance of life, Caine's closing hours expressed only one facet of vibrance, a giving son, friend and brother. In the spectrum of life and loss, love and loss, and premature of his contribution, Caine was at the precipice of manhood. Rare in spirit and irreplaceable, Caine's final candle lit a view one could not have envisioned except through him in loss, a view of another place, and hope from the shadows to the sun.

Spring Thaw

When God's hand comes down and takes you away
Puts you so far out wide in an instant one day
And the losses you count from all that was yours
Whilst your heart goes numb from the hurt that is caused
As the ice sets in you look away all you like
For the joy of day, and delight of night, is lost

Winter sets in the chill in the air
The heart wrenching pain of years of despair
You cannot go forward nor can you go back
The prayers for direction become your stack
Of embers of hope, a place you can serve
To give all you can, when, your prayers are heard!

For one day, from somewhere out of the blue
There is a man standing in front of you
From the Emperors Waltz or the Blue Danube
Or the Spanish Matador with a red rose too
Comes a jolt of the heart and a flutter within
Your spirit soars to the man that is him
His essence glows and into his heat
Your souls become one and winter retreats

By whose perspective is it a sin
To desire, to love, another human being
To hold in your heart, your body to impart
To reach, to touch, an essence that is such
To give all you can to this remarkable man, who isn't yours

With the thaw of spring, a new joy begins
And the precious gift from God forever stays within
As your body melts and can give again
There is hope for life and renewal in a spring thaw

Heart Strings

How far do you go, how far can we part
How much can we stretch the pain of a heart

Some hold it ever so deep within
Some keep it closer to surface of skin

Some know its texture, some know its scent
Most know its sound when in deep repent

How bright its light, the sun in my day
Being you brings joy in remarkable ways
So may I say

Distance is only as far as the heart
And life is truly precious

A Lover's Blush

A moment's glance
A heated flush
Her fingers search the velvet brush
Of petals deep, they take within
The ardent touch of her soft skin

Lost in scent her senses reel
Her feet beneath she cannot feel
She hides the lush of love within
Breaking through her kitty grin

Whilst sweet perfume consumes the air
He reaches past her tousled hair
And gently turns to him her chin
He thanks her for the rose

Sparkle In My Heart

From night to day and day to night
Thoughts of you become the light
And the sparkle in my heart
Brightens to a smile

So I breathe it in again
To hear thoughts of you again
Which light the sparkle in my heart
And keep me warm
In thoughts of you again

Whispers of Truth

In my voice I heard
I will keep you in my prayers
And in my heart I felt
How very much I love you

I will fight you
I will fight with you
I will fight for you
Because I love you

Because I love you unconditionally
I will stand aside
So you may grow

Truth liberates

When we live in truth others can live their truth
And we may all find our destiny...................

LORNA LEILANII was born and raised in the cultural foundations of Papua New Guinea and Maoridom. Steeped in spiritual sensitivity through her corridor of growth Lorna acquired the unique capacity of an empath. A portal for the expression of others entering through her nightscapes, daytime hustles, and quiet contemplations, maturity has finally released her gift of acknowledgement to give flight to their 'WHISPERS OF TRUTH'.

In our dance of life, as precious as love, are our friendships. Caroline, Dolores, Jeanny, and Vavine - Thank you ♥.

CPSIA information can be obtained
at www.ICGtesting.com
Printed in the USA
BVHW020840070819
555302BV00003B/23/P

* 9 7 8 1 5 1 4 4 9 4 7 0 7 *